"This little gem of a book, written in very brief chapters, reflects the gleanings of Sid's years of reflection on God's word, especially the Psalms, in regard to a wide range of real-life struggles. No scripture-as-recipe-book with facile answers here, but rather a starting place to provoke the dialogue of faith."

—BART GROOMS
Pastoral Counselor

"Sid Burgess is an excellent preacher and a thoughtful liturgist who leads a creative, loving congregation. This book gives us what that congregation has experienced for years: insightful, imaginative appropriation of Holy Scripture for life's countless challenges . . . Each page carefully reminds us of the good news in Jesus Christ—God is truly for us."

—JOSEPH SCRIVNER
University Professor

Scripture Apps Made Easy

Scripture Apps Made Easy

Biblical Applications for Today's Tough Times

SID BURGESS

RESOURCE *Publications* · Eugene, Oregon

SCRIPTURE APPS MADE EASY
Biblical Applications for Today's Tough Times

Resource Publications
An Imprint of Wipf and Stock Publishers
199 W. 8th Ave., Suite 3
Eugene, OR 97401

www.wipfandstock.com

ISBN 13: 978-1-61097-790-6

For Melissa

Contents

Foreword

SEVERAL YEARS ago, Rev. Sid Burgess created an alternative worship service for those who struggled with the traditional Mother's Day church format. Sid, along with his wife Melissa, designed a sensitive and creative healing service for the afternoon of Mother's Day. This took place at Edgewood Presbyterian Church in Birmingham, Alabama. I was delighted to be the preacher that day. Following a Southern tradition of wearing red roses to honor living mothers and white ones for the deceased, we placed a pink rose on the pulpit to represent those struggling with loss, miscarriage, SIDS, infertility, and broken dreams. I recall this service as I write because Sid Burgess "stepped into a gap" in ministry—a gap filled with pain, retrospection, and "the big hurt."

Once again, Sid Burgess has "stepped into a ministerial gap" by writing *Scripture Apps Made Easy*. He is offering alternative avenues or apps (applications) for the many big hurts in life. These include aging, Alzheimer's Disease, bullying, doubt, heart surgery, obesity, surgery, unemployment, violence, and many more. Each concise chapter offers appropriate scripture for the pain that is faced.

In times of stress, it is the nature of humankind to fall back on the familiar. In this handbook, Sid Burgess offers to the pastor or lay minister a selection of familiar scriptures to comfort the suffering. It is a handy, humane resource and reference. In addition, in places of disaster and in times of shock, the minister herself or himself may be almost immobilized. Again, this manual offers a way to move forward in ministry.

There is a phase of ministerial development when clergy move into a place of wisdom. That is one of the descriptions of a pastor: a wise man or wise woman. In this contribution, *Scripture Apps Made Easy*, Sid Burgess has not only "stepped into the gap of literature," he has grounded himself in the wisdom of the ages.

Jeanne Stevenson-Moessner, DTh
Professor of Pastoral Care, Perkins School of Theology,
Southern Methodist University
Fellow, American Association of Pastoral Counselors
Ordained minister, PCUSA

Preface

"WHY DOESN'T God talk to us like God talks to people in the Bible?" the child asked her mother. Though the answer may not satisfy the child, people of faith believe that God does speak to us—present tense—through Holy Scripture. This is not to say that God is limited to scripture, but the church has long held that God speaks most clearly through the ancient texts passed down to us by our Hebrew ancestors and the first-century Christian community. In addition, the Bible gives us the words to address God directly with our hopes and our hurts, our dreams and our fears. The purpose of this book is to make a precious few relevant texts readily accessible to you.

I have used the New Revised Standard Version (NRSV) almost exclusively here. However, it was published just before the larger church became sensitive to the need for more inclusive language when referring to Holy God. Therefore, you will often find the word *God* in brackets [ ]. That is to signal that I have changed a male pronoun, normally *he*, to the word *God*, inasmuch as God is neither male nor female, but Spirit. In deference to the NRSV translators and to avoid repetition, I have not done this in every case, but often enough, I hope, that the reader will become accustomed to thinking of God without gender identification. You will also note that I have used several texts repeatedly, but not to worry, as none of these texts can be worn out.

Acknowledgments

I WANT to express my appreciation

to the members and friends of Edgewood Presbyterian Church who have so graciously and openly allowed me to share their hurts and their hopes, their joys and their sorrows for more than twenty years;

to those individuals who have given me permission to use their personal stories;

to Walter Brueggemann, who first opened to me the depth and breadth of the book of Psalms and who, twenty years later, encouraged the publication of this collection of scriptures, which draws largely from "the prayer book of ancient Israel";

to my colleagues in ministry who have affirmed my use of scripture in pastoral care;

to selected friends and associates who kindly read parts of the manuscript in its various stages of development and offered wise counsel; and

to my faithful and loving wife, Melissa, who not only encouraged this project from the outset but also stepped up to serve as a wise and resourceful editor.

INTRODUCTION

The Bible Has an App for Cancer

"I DIDN'T know the Bible said anything about cancer," the patient exclaimed. She had been diagnosed with breast cancer and was soon to begin that onerous regimen of radiation and chemotherapy. I had just read to her this excerpt from the book of Psalms:

> Depart from me, all you [cancer cells],
> for the LORD has heard the sound of my weeping.
> (Ps 6:8)

Of course, the biblical text has "workers of evil" instead of "cancer cells," but certainly a deadly cancer qualifies as a worker of evil. Here was a clear biblical application—a scripture app in today's technical shorthand—for this woman's medical crisis. For others of us, our crisis, our "cancer," may be a painful memory that will not fade, a wound that will not heal, an illness that cannot be cured, a broken relationship that cannot be restored, a career that cannot be put back on track, an addiction that cannot be overcome. Whatever the source of the pain, I contend there is a scripture app for it. The biblical writers have provided us with stories, poems, and prayers that give us the words to express our anguish to God, and divine assurance that God is listening and that our ultimate rescue and redemption is assured.

The problem is, even the most devoted people of faith often have a very limited biblical repertoire—just a handful of psalms; the Beatitudes, perhaps; for weddings, 1 Corinthians 13; and for funerals, Psalm 23. As a pastor I have had access to the pastor's edition of the Presbyterian Church (U.S.A.)'s *Book of Common Worship*, which offers a number of excerpts from scripture for use in pastoral care. I carry this handy resource with me whenever I make a pastoral call, be it in the home, hospital, or funeral home. But I have often found its small collection of verses too limiting. I have longed for a more extensive, though still convenient, resource—perhaps one that I could even put into the hands of parishioners and friends. This desire brought this project into being.

Of course, many devotional books and other resources cite book, chapter, and verse. But following the format of the *Book of Common Worship*, this book provides the text itself rather than a citation. With the text in hand, we have the words to report our hurts directly to Holy God.

> When the cares of my heart are many,
> [God's] consolations cheer my soul.
> (Ps 94:19)

To be sure, the topics listed here exhaust neither human dilemmas nor biblical resources. But these are among the most common issues in my life and in the lives of those I have sought to serve through more than twenty years of pastoral experience. Drawing on these experiences, I have provided brief commentary on each topic in the hopes of demonstrating just how relevant God's Word can be in times of distress.

Finally, I want to offer a word about my theological perspective. In response to loss, people who mean well often tell us, "God has a plan," or, "This happened to fulfill a divine purpose," or, simply, "Everything happens for a reason." Maybe so, but in my view, God does not play human beings like puppets. As I read scripture, the God of justice and mercy would never be the source of injustice or misery for God's people. However, the Bible does assure us there is no situation out of which God cannot work good for God's people. As Joseph tells the brothers who sold him into slavery,

> Even though you intended to do harm to me,
> God intended it for good.
> (Gen 50:20)

Shalom!
Sid Burgess

Accidents and the Emergency Room

ACCIDENTS HAPPEN and, contrary to popular perception, God does not cause them. Quite the contrary, as the beloved Psalm 121 assures us:

> The Lord is your keeper;
> the Lord is your shade at your right hand.
> The sun shall not strike you by day,
> nor the moon by night.
> The Lord will keep you from all evil;
> [God] will keep your life.
> (Ps 121:5–7)

Even so, we human beings are susceptible to mishaps. Best laid plans go awry. Equipment fails. Mortals make mistakes. Headlines go to airplane crashes, train wrecks, and automobile accidents, but most accidents happen at home. And the most frequent of all is a fall.

When my mother, then recently widowed, saw a critter scamper across the den floor she leaped from her chair armed with a rolled up newspaper and gave chase. In the flash of an eye she was tumbling, head over heels, down steep basement steps. Both wrists were shattered. Only by the hardest effort was she able to summon help.

> The Lord upholds all who are falling,
> and raises up all who are bowed down.
> (Ps 145:14)

Help came and my mother was rushed to the nearest hospital, where she waited what seemed an interminable period of time to see a surgeon who could set her broken bones. When God's people are hurting, the prophet Jeremiah assures us that God is hurting. While injured and ill people wait impatiently, God grows impatient, too:

> For the hurt of my poor people I am hurt,
> I mourn, and dismay has taken hold of me.
> Is there no balm in Gilead?
> Is there no physician there?
> Why then has the health of my poor people
> not been restored?
> (Jer 8:21–22)

So, what is God going to do when emergency strikes? I cite this verse when I arrive at the emergency room:

> For [God] will hide me in his shelter
> in the day of trouble;
> [God] will conceal me under the cover of his tent;
> he will set me high on a rock.
> (Ps 27:5)

For shelter God is providing a hospital or clinic. For a tent, God provides the curtains of an examination room. Instead of a high rock, God provides a much softer hospital bed, for "these words are trustworthy and true" (Rev 21:5).

Aging

ONE OF my beloved parishioners often told me: "Growing old is hell." We Americans are living longer, which can be a mixed blessing. Yes, we have every hope of seeing our grandchildren grow up, but the reality is that we are not likely to be pain-free witnesses. We would all like to sit proud and erect in the saddle as we ride off into the sunset. But the reality is far more likely to be extended home health care, assisted living, nursing home, or hospital, with the attendant loss of options, privacy, and control. Psalm 71 offers this prayer for us:

> In you, O LORD, I take refuge;
> let me never be put to shame. . . .
> Be to me a rock of refuge,
> a strong fortress, to save me,
> for you are my rock and my fortress.
> (Ps 71:1, 3)

As the old revival song proclaims, "all other ground is sinking sand." Psalm 71 reminds us that as long as we have breath, we have a mission, a calling to proclaim God's might to the next generation:

> Do not cast me off in the time of old age;
> do not forsake me when my strength is spent. . . .
> So even to old age and gray hairs,
> O God, do not forsake me,
> until I proclaim your might
> to all the generations to come.
> (Ps 71:9, 18)

Alcoholism and Addiction

Substance abuse is epidemic in our time. As God once offered instruction to Moses, God may be heard today commanding, "Let my people go," to our addictions.

> Then the LORD said to Moses, "Go to Pharaoh and say to him, 'Thus says the Lord: Let my people go, so that they may worship me.'"
> (Exod 8:1; also 5:1; 7:16; 8:20, etc.)

In biblical language the people of God are often "strangers in a foreign land." They frequently find themselves out-of-place and vulnerable, in situations that have caused many in our time to succumb to drink or drugs, gambling or sex. First Peter advises an entirely different response to our loneliness:

> Beloved, I urge you as aliens and exiles
> to abstain from the desires of the flesh
> that wage war against the soul.
> Conduct yourselves honorably among the Gentiles,
> so that, though they malign you as evil doers,
> they may see your honorable deeds
> and glorify God when he comes to judge.
> (1 Pet 2:11–12)

ON ENTERING REHAB

When a dear friend entered rehab recently, he went by way of the hospital's mental health unit. He was required to remove all of his clothes and don paper-thin hospital attire. Upon entering the secured unit he heard the door lock behind him and thought, then and there, that life as he knew it was over. Would that he had been able to summon this sacred assurance:

> For surely I know the plans I have for you,
> says the LORD,
> plans for your welfare and not for harm,
> to give you a future with hope.
> (Jer 29:11)

ON COMPLETING REHAB

Breaking the bonds of addiction is often a "battle royal," requiring an "army" of doctors, mental health professionals, and physical therapists, aided by spiritual counselors, social workers, friends, and family members. When the battle is won, the prophet Isaiah leads the victory celebration:

> Comfort, O comfort my people, says your God.
> Speak tenderly to Jerusalem,
> and cry to her that she has served her term,
> that her penalty is paid,
> that she has received from the LORD's hand
> double for all her sins.
> (Isa 40:1–2)

ON THE BATTLE TO STAY "CLEAN"

Alcoholics for Christ (alcoholicsforchrist.com) points its members to this promise from Isaiah:

Thus says your Sovereign, the LORD,
your God who pleads the cause of his people:
See, I have taken from your hand the cup of staggering;
you shall drink no more
from the bowl of my wrath.
(Isa 51:22)

The same group cites the testimony of John the Baptist at his first encounter with Jesus, "Here is the Lamb of God who takes away the sin of the world" (John 1:29), and the declaration of Jesus later in the Gospel, "So if the Son makes you free, you will be free indeed" (John 8:36).

Alzheimer's Disease

LIVING LEGEND Pat Summit, who has led the University of Tennessee women's basketball team to eight national championships, was diagnosed with early-onset dementia, Alzheimer's type, at the age of 59. She went to the famed Mayo Clinic reporting symptoms of erratic behavior, bewilderment, and fear. She came away with a diagnosis that at first had her angry and depressed.

The name Alzheimer's was unknown to the ancients, but they surely knew the effects of dementia. In the Gospel of John, the Risen Jesus reminds his disciples:

> Very truly, I tell you, when you were younger,
> you used to fasten your own belt
> and to go wherever you wished.
> But when you grow old,
> you will stretch out your hands,
> and someone else will fasten a belt around you
> and take you where you do not wish to go.
> (John 21:18)

Coach Summit is not one to take any challenge lying down. She has a game plan to battle this condition with medication and mental exercises. For now, she has no trouble making her needs known. When the day comes that she is not able to do that, Psalm 139 provides this prayer, assuring us that God knows our needs before we ask:

O LORD, you have searched me and known me.
You know when I sit down and when I rise up;
you discern my thoughts from far away.
You search out my path and my lying down,
and are acquainted with all my ways.
Even before a word is on my tongue,
O LORD, you know it completely.
(Ps 139:1–4)

Arrest and Incarceration

THE COUNTY jail and the state prison are the least "user-friendly" places a pastor ever visits. All the surfaces are hard, and all the doors are loud. Everyone is restricted, if not restrained. Prisoners, jailers, and visitors alike are locked into clear confines. No one moves from point A to point B without assistance or permission. And this is the perspective from the outside. One can only imagine how harsh it is inside, where the coffee is always cold, the food is bland, the space is crowded, and the company troublesome at best, dangerous at worst.

> Some sat in darkness and in gloom,
> prisoners in misery and in irons,
> for they had rebelled against the words of God,
> and spurned the counsel of the Most High.
> Their hearts were bowed down with hard labor;
> they fell down, with no one to help.
> (Ps 107:10–12)

When a person runs afoul of the law, he or she starts a chain reaction among family members and victims that can have harmful repercussions for a generation or longer. In the United Sates, with the highest documented incarceration rate in the world, a lot of families are hurting. For prisoners and their families Psalm 107 offers this vision of hope:

Then they cried to the LORD in their trouble,
and [God] saved them from their distress;
he brought them out of darkness and gloom,
and broke their bonds asunder.
Let them thank the LORD for his steadfast love,
for [God's] wonderful works to humankind.
(Ps 107:13–15)

Arthritis

M ARTHA, WITH beautiful, long, snow-white hair, was the first person to tell me about "Arthur." She was in her nineties and living in a nursing home when I came to know her. She suffered from chronic arthritis, which she described as mice gnawing on her bones. When I would read this verse from Psalm 31, she would say, "That's it, that's Arthur come a-calling!"

> For my life is spent with sorrow,
> and my years with sighing;
> my strength fails because of my misery,
> and my bones waste away.
> (Ps 31:10)

The author of Psalm 102 may also have suffered from something like arthritis:

> For my days pass away like smoke,
> and my bones burn like a furnace.
> (Ps 102:3)

Unlike the ancients, we do have medications that can provide some relief to this crippling condition. When those medications fail to lessen the pain, we still have this word of sacred assurance: "for I will contend with those who contend with you" (Isa 49:25c).

Betrayal

FROM JESUS to the kids at school, everyone—at one time or another—has experienced the sting of betrayal. The closer the confidant, the deeper the hurt, as Psalm 55 clearly knows:

> It is not enemies who taunt me—
> I could bear that;
> it is not adversaries who deal insolently with me—
> I could hide from them.
> But it is you, my equal,
> my companion, my familiar friend,
> with whom I kept pleasant company;
> we walked in the house of God with the throng.
> (Ps 55:12–14)

The poet seems to know quite well how duplicity works:

> With speech smoother than butter,
> but with a heart set on war;
> with words that were softer than oil,
> but in fact were drawn swords.
> (Ps 55:21)

Nevertheless, when tongues are wagging, Psalm 55 offers this wise counsel:

> Cast your burden on the LORD,
> and he will sustain you;
> [God] will never permit
> the righteous to be moved.
> (Ps 55:22)

Bullying

ONE OF the most prominent bullies in the Bible is the huge Philistine warrior Goliath, who gets his comeuppance from the young shepherd boy David. But Goliath's demise is by no means the end of bullying—not in the Bible, certainly not in life.

For fourteen-year-old Jamey Rodemeyer of Williamsville, New York, the taunts came not from some distant giant but from his peers. Jamey took his life in September 2011, after what his parents claim was years of bullying because of struggles with his sexuality. In a YouTube video Jamey said the kids a school were telling him he was "going to hell" because he was gay.

Unfortunately, the bullying to which Jamey was subjected is by no means isolated. A recent study by the California Safe Schools Coalition found that nearly half of California students who identify as lesbian, gay, or bisexual have been the victims of gender-based harassment.

The prophet Isaiah assures us that bullies do not operate under divine mandate: "If anyone stirs up strife, it is not from me." What's more, the prophet promises, "Whoever stirs up strife with you shall fall because of you" (Isa 54:15).

The reformed bully, St. Paul, offers this encouragement to victims of harassment:

> Suffering produces endurance,
> and endurance produces character,

and character produces hope,
and hope does not disappoint us,
because God's love has been poured into our hearts
through the Holy Spirit that has been given to us.
(Rom 5:3–5)

With this hope, victims of bullying, especially bullying that stems from gender, sexual, religious, or racial bias, do not have to take the taunts lying down. Instead, we are offered this prayer to urge God to take up our defense:

Contend, O LORD, with those who contend with me;
fight against those who fight against me!
Take hold of shield and buckler,
and rise up to help me!
Draw the spear and javelin
against my pursuers;
say to my soul, "I am your salvation."
Let them be put to shame and dishonor
who seek after my life.
Let them be turned back and confounded
who devise evil against me.
Let them be like chaff before the wind,
with the angel of the LORD driving them on.
Let their way be dark and slippery,
with the angel of the LORD pursuing them.
(Ps 35:1–6)

Cancer

DIAGNOSIS

"Looks to me like melanoma," the dermatologist said. I was stunned. "Not to worry," she continued, "we'll remove this ugly little fellow and do a biopsy. We'll call and let you know."

What I heard was, "Better get your affairs in order!" Cancer is just that frightening. The ancients did not have our name for this disease, but they surely knew our fear, leaving us this prayer:

> O Lord, heal me, for my bones are shaking with terror.
> My soul is struck with terror,
> while you, O Lord—how long?
> (Ps 6:2–3)

Fortunately for me, my scare proved to be a false alarm. But for too many friends and loved ones, the dread diagnosis has been all too accurate. The American Cancer Society says about 1,500 Americans die from this disease every day. Psalm 6 goes on to describe a day—and a night—in the life of anyone who is battling any form of cancer.

> I am weary with my moaning;
> every night I flood my bed with tears;
> I drench my couch with my weeping.

My eyes waste away because of grief;
they grow weak because of all my foes.
Depart from me, all you workers of evil,
for the Lord has heard the sound of my weeping.
(Ps 6:6–8)

TREATMENT

The twin treatments of chemotherapy and radiation can put the "bad guys" to flight, but the side effects are often debilitating. Psalm 69 seems to know something about a cure than can seem almost as bad as the disease:

Save me, O God,
for the waters have come up to my neck.
I sink in deep mire,
where there is no foothold;
I have come into deep waters,
and the flood sweeps over me.
I am weary with my crying;
my throat is parched.
My eyes grow dim
with waiting for my God.
(Ps 69:1–3)

People of faith believe our living God is at work through the medical and scientific community to find a cure for cancer. Survival rates are on the rise, and Psalm 121 assures us that God will not sleep until a cure is found:

I lift up my eyes to the hills—
from where will my help come?
My help comes from the Lord,
who made heaven and earth.

[God] will not let your foot be moved;
he who keeps you will not slumber.
He who keeps Israel
will neither slumber nor sleep.
(Ps 121:1–4)

Change and Uncertainty

ONCE THERE were only two certainties in life: death and taxes. Now there are three: death, taxes, and change. Technology changes so swiftly these days that even the most tech savvy among us have trouble keeping up. In the corporate world, structures and strategies seem to be in a constant state of flux. In education, teaching methods and resources change. In medicine, there are always new procedures, new medications; in government, new rules and regulations; and, at church, new music and worship styles. In the midst of this sea of change, scripture urges:

> Be strong and courageous;
> do not be frightened or dismayed,
> for the LORD your God is with you wherever you go.
> (Josh 1:9)

And here is more from Psalm 46:

> The nations are in an uproar, the kingdoms totter;
> [God] utters his voice, the earth melts.
> The LORD of hosts is with us;
> the God of Jacob [and Rachel and Leah] is our refuge.
> (Ps 46:6–7)

In the face of any uncertainty, here is a prayer to bring to the forefront:

Be pleased, O God, to deliver me.
O LORD, make haste to help me! . . .
You are my help and my deliverer;
O LORD, do not delay!
(Ps 70:1, 5b)

Chronic Pain

A LOAD of topsoil introduced me to chronic pain when I was just thirty years old. The driver dumped the dirt at our curb, collected my check, and departed long before I realized that the topsoil came mixed with heavy clay. With a wheelbarrow and a shovel I tried to move that mountain of heavy dirt. The result was a severely strained back. Over the course of many tortured months, I came to more fully appreciate the term, *debilitating*. Painkillers and muscle relaxers did not put a dent in the pain, which eventually got so bad I could not concentrate at work. Psalm 3 describes my desperation:

> O Lord, how many are my foes!
> Many are rising against me;
> many are saying to me,
> "There is no help for you in God."
> (Ps 3:1–2)

The psalmist, however, is not easily discouraged. Verse three of this psalm begins with what biblical scholars call the biggest word in faith: *but.*

> But you, O Lord, are a shield around me,
> my glory, and the one who lifts up my head.
> I cry aloud to the Lord,
> and [God] answers me from his holy hill.
> (Ps 3:3–4)

God answered me through a rheumatologist who prescribed a TENS unit, a transcutaneous electronic nerve stimulator. For a year and a half I wore that device to mask the pain while my body healed. Countless others are not so fortunate. For those who still suffer chronic pain, Isaiah's "Suffering Servant" assures us that God suffers along with us:

> Surely he has borne our infirmities
> and carried our diseases.
> (Isa 53:4)

Dealing with Difficult People

THE MOVIES, TV shows, and crime novels depict the bad guys slithering through the city under the cover of darkness. But we are more likely to encounter them in the workplace as managers, supervisors, and coworkers who just seem to have a spiteful spirit. They can make our lives miserable. Psalm 52 has their number:

> Why do you boast, O mighty one,
> of mischief done against the godly?
> All day long you are plotting destruction.
> Your tongue is like a sharp razor,
> you worker of treachery.
> You love evil more than good,
> and lying more than speaking the truth.
> You love all words that devour,
> O deceitful tongue.
> (Ps 52:1–4)

However, Psalm 52 also has this sacred promise for the "bad guys":

> But God will break you down forever;
> [God] will snatch and tear you from your tent;
> [God] will uproot you from the land of the living.
> (Ps 52:5)

And Ps 52 holds out this promise for the "good guys":

> But I am like a green olive tree
> in the house of God.
> I trust in the steadfast love of God
> forever and ever.
> (Ps 52:8)

Still, the question remains: What to do about our anger? Psalm 37 gives us this advice:

> Refrain from anger, and forsake wrath.
> Do not fret—it leads only to evil.
> For the wicked shall be cut off,
> but those who wait for the LORD shall inherit the land.
> (Ps 37:8–9)

Perhaps even more helpful is this wise counsel from Psalm 7, urging us to let God handle our fury.

> Rise up, O LORD, in your anger;
> lift yourself up against the fury of my enemies.
> (Ps 7:6a)

And Psalm 31 offers this assurance of ultimate resolution:

> The LORD preserves the faithful,
> but abundantly repays the one who acts haughtily.
> Be strong, and let your heart take courage,
> all you who wait for the LORD.
> (Ps 31:23b–24)

Death

OFTEN DEATH—AND sometimes life, too—seems like a trapdoor that opens beneath us, dropping us or someone we love into the great unknown. This verse assures us that "underneath are the everlasting arms":

> The eternal God is your refuge
> and underneath are the everlasting arms.
> (Deut 33:27 [NIV])

When life hangs in the balance, nothing comforts quite like this sacred assurance from St. Paul:

> If we live, we live to the LORD,
> and if we die, we die to the LORD;
> so then, whether we live or whether we die,
> we are the LORD's.
> (Rom 14:8)

Next, I like to hear St. Paul thundering through the ages with this powerful affirmation:

> For I am convinced that neither death, nor life,
> nor angels, nor rulers,
> nor things present, nor things to come,
> nor powers, nor height, nor depth,
> nor anything else in all creation,
> will be able to separate us
> from the love of God in Christ Jesus our LORD.
> (Rom 8:38–39)

Once the shock of death has begun to recede we are often left with nagging questions: "Now what?" "What about me?" "What am I to do?" "How shall I go forward?" When these questions arise, the prophet Isaiah delivers this divine pledge:

> Do not fear, for I am with you,
> do not be afraid, for I am your God;
> I will strengthen you, I will help you,
> I will uphold you with my victorious right hand.
> (Isa 41:10)

Finally, when a person dies short of the divinely authorized "three-score-and-ten," Isaiah assures us that this is not the divine intention:

> No more shall there be in it
> an infant that lives but a few days,
> or an old person who does not live out a lifetime.
> (Isa 65:20)

Depression

You would think a pastor would be the last person in the world to suffer depression. After all, he or she is "surrounded by so great a cloud of witnesses" (Heb 12:1)—faithful members of a loving congregation, plus supportive clergy colleagues. He or she is immersed in God's Holy Word, where divine hope is offered even in the valley of dry bones (see Ezek 37:1–6). But clinical depression does not recognize such boundaries. When years of good counseling, spiritual direction, and personal study failed to lift me "up from the desolate pit, out of the miry bog" (Ps 40:2), I sought medical help, as the poet of Israel urges:

> While I kept silence, my body wasted away,
> through my groaning all day long.
> (Ps 32:3)

The ancients knew quite well the debilitating impact of depression:

> The human spirit will endure sickness;
> but a broken spirit—who can bear?
> (Prov 18:14)

In our time, depression seems to be a national epidemic. The website, depression-help-resource.com, lists a host of famous people who have dealt with this condition, including actor Jim Carrey, comedienne Ellen DeGeneres, singer Sheryl Crowe, Hall of Fame quarterback Terry

Bradshaw, novelist William Styron, and political spouses Tipper Gore and Kitty Dukakis.

Psalm 77 gives voice to the crisis in faith that depression often generates:

> Has [God's] steadfast love ceased forever?
> Are his promises at an end for all time?
> Has God forgotten to be gracious?
> Has [God] in anger shut up his compassion?
> (Ps 77:8–9)

Having openly questioned God, the poet then offers this way forward through the darkness:

> I will call to mind the deeds of the LORD;
> I will remember your wonders of old.
> I will meditate on all your work,
> and muse on your mighty deeds.
> (Ps 77:11–12)

Psalm 94 offers this testimony of divine deliverance:

> If the LORD had not been my help,
> my soul would soon have lived in the land of silence.
> When I thought, "My foot is slipping,"
> your steadfast love, O LORD, held me up.
> When the cares of my heart are many,
> your consolations cheer my soul.
> (Ps 94:17–19)

Despair

A FRIEND recently wrote, "My life is such drudgery, it is nearly unspeakable." Medical maladies pile on top of financial woes, and job stress compounds family dysfunction. The ancient poet of Israel seems to have "been there, done that."

> Be gracious to me, O LORD, for I am in distress;
> my eye wastes away from grief,
> my soul and body also.
> For my life is spent with sorrow,
> and my years with sighing;
> my strength fails because of my misery,
> and my bones waste away.
> I am the scorn of all my adversaries,
> a horror to my neighbors,
> an object of dread to my acquaintances;
> those who see me in the street flee from me.
> I have passed out of mind like one who is dead;
> I have become like a broken vessel.
> (Ps 31:9–12)

Some people will tell you God does not want to hear your complaints. Psalm 31 counters that false assertion as it continues:

> But I trust in you, O LORD;
> I say, "You are my God."

> My times are in your hand;
> deliver me from the hand of my enemies and
> persecutors.
> Let your face shine upon your servant;
> save me in your steadfast love.
> (Ps 31:14–16)

Psalm 31 and similar passages remain in our tradition to document that life is difficult and that God is willing to listen to all of our complaints. What's more, notice to whom the psalm is addressed: "In you, O Lord, I seek refuge" (v. 1). This prayer is addressed to the One whom the psalmist believes will ultimately provide help.

Diabetes

TYPE 1

For Katie, diagnosed at age eight, it took quite some time for the significance this disorder to sink in. She writes, "Two years after being diagnosed, I remember sitting in my mother's lap, and looking down at my hands, and asking myself, 'Why me? Why do I have to carry this disease?'"

Katie is not alone in living either with this condition or with her questions. The American Diabetes Association reports that about one in every four hundred children and adolescents in the United States, about 215,000 people under the age of twenty, have diabetes. Many of them are surely asking questions too—questions that seem to echo the Bible's Psalm 22:

> My God, my God, why have you forsaken me?
> Why are you so far from helping me,
> from the words of my groaning?
> O my God, I cry by day, but you do not answer;
> and by night, but find no rest.
> (Ps 22:1–2)

It surely is not the divine intention for any child to suffer this disease: "Let the little children come to me; do not stop them," Jesus said, "for it is to such as these that the

33

kingdom of God belongs" (Mark 10:14). The God of abiding love and evenhanded justice would never assign some children to wealth and the vast majority to poverty; some to good health and far too many to no health care at all; some to competent and devoted parents, while leaving legions of others to fend for themselves. Even so, God can use this disease and other maladies for good, as Katie has discovered. Now a high school senior, Katie writes, "I look in the mirror and I see that I am a stronger and more independent person because of diabetes. Diabetes [has] made me resilient."

What's more, people of faith believe that God is at work through thousands of nurses, doctors, and scientists seeking more effective treatment and, ultimately, a cure. "We will cure diabetes," says Dr. Camillo Ricordi of the Diabetes Research Institute. "This is not a prediction; it is a promise."

TYPE 2

Ken Smith is a giant of a man with a powerful voice but a gentle spirit. It takes a lot to make him angry, but a diagnosis of Type 2 diabetes did just that. His initial response was both anger—"Damn it all"—and denial: "That can't be right." After all, he was a God-fearing, church-going, hardworking, faithful and loving husband, dad, and granddad. Ken made a stop at each of the normal stages of grief, including self-pity: "Why me?"; depression: "I'm on the road to the grave"; and resignation: "I guess it's just going to have to be this way." With the support of a loving family and a good medical team, Ken has surfaced with determination: "I'm going to beat this thing."

> For surely I know the plans I have for you, says the
> Lord, plans for your welfare and not for harm, to give
> you a future with hope.
> (Jer 29:11)

If current trends continue, an astonishing one of every three U.S. adults will have diabetes by 2050. The Centers for Disease Control and Prevention says Type 2 can be prevented or delayed by the twin disciplines of diet and exercise. To start, "Eat your veggies!" The CDC urges a low-calorie, low-fat eating plan, which is also the divine diet prescribed in Genesis: "See, I have given you every plant yielding seed that is upon the face of all the earth, and every tree with seed in its fruit; you shall have them for food" (Gen 1:29).

To continue, exercise regularly. The CDC urges building up to thirty minutes of physical activity, five days a week. God says you can do this! "When you walk, your step will not be hampered; and if you run, you will not stumble" (Prov 4:12).

For divine support, the prophet Isaiah offers this prayer: "Oh, restore me to health and make me live" (Isa 38:16b).

Diagnosis

WHEN THE doctor says, "We need to do some tests," warning bells begin to ring in our heads. "Tests for what?" we ask. "What you are looking for?" "What makes you think there is a serious problem?"

Waiting for the results of those tests can be agonizing. Is it cancer? Is it malignant or benign? Has it spread? Is it operable? Or, once again, am I making a mountain out of the proverbial molehill? Am I turning a bad cold or an upset stomach into a fatal illness? In either case and in all cases, Psalm 27 offers these words of assurance:

> The LORD is the light of my salvation;
> whom shall I fear?
> The LORD is the stronghold of my life;
> of whom shall I be afraid?
> (Ps 27:1)

When the diagnosis is good, Psalm 86 gives us words to express our gratitude to God:

> I give thanks to you, O LORD my God,
> with my whole heart,
> and I will glorify your name forever.
> For great is your steadfast love toward me.
> (Ps 86:12–13)

When the diagnosis is discouraging, the prophet Isaiah assures us that help is on the way:

> Do not fear, for I am with you,
> do not be afraid, for I am your God;
> I will strengthen you, I will help you,
> I will uphold you with my victorious right hand.
> (Isa 41:10)

When the diagnosis says our time for departure is at hand, our days are numbered, here is sacred assurance from Isaiah:

> When you pass through the waters, I will be with you;
> and through the rivers, they shall not overwhelm you;
> when you walk through fire you shall not be burned,
> and the flame shall not consume you.
> For I am the LORD your God,
> the Holy One of Israel, your Savior.
> (Isa 43:2–3)

Disability and Loss of Ability

DISABILITY

A<small>N ASTONISHING</small> 36 million Americans, or about 12 percent of all children and adults, have disabilities. The disability can involve any one of the following: hearing, vision, cognition, mobility, self-care, or independent living. During my seminary days I had a friend who suffered all of the above. "Linda" drove the "pace car"—a motorized wheelchair—on our evening walks. Linda required the use of a wheelchair because she suffered with cerebral palsy. Her speech was often slurred and her limbs curled. She described painful seizures, sensitivity to touch, and frequent falls. I asked Linda how she coped with the pain of this chronic condition. She said she cried herself to sleep every night, reading the words of Psalm 88. Here are excerpts:

> For my soul is full of troubles,
> and my life draws near to [Death].
> I am counted among those who go down to the Pit;
> I am like those who have no help,
> like those forsaken among the dead,
> like the slain that lie in the grave,
> like those whom you remember no more.
> (Ps 88:3–5)

While people of faith know the God of goodness and love cannot be the source of pain and agony, Psalm 88 essentially says that when there is no one else to blame, God will accept responsibility:

> You have put me in the depths of the Pit,
> in the regions dark and deep.
> Your wrath lies heavy upon me,
> and you overwhelm me with all your waves.
> (Ps 88:6–7)

Linda told me that her limited mobility, plus frequent accidents and illnesses, left her isolated, as Psalm 88 seems to understand:

> You have caused my companions to shun me;
> you have made me a thing of horror to them.
> I am shut in so that I cannot escape;
> my eye grows dim through sorrow.
> (Ps 88:8–9)

With the help of Psalm 88, Linda was able to vent her anger and frustration to Holy God:

> O LORD, why do you cast me off?
> Why do you hide your face from me?
> Wretched and close to death from my youth up,
> I suffer your terrors; I am desperate.
> (Ps 88:14–15)

Having accepted God's invitation to be honest—"let my prayer come before you" (v. 2)—Linda would eventually get to sleep, most nights. She slept with Psalm 88's assurance that when morning came, God would still be there with her, listening when no one else would:

> But I, O LORD, cry out to you;
> in the morning my prayer comes before you.
> (Ps 88:13)

LOSS OF ABILITY

When my wife, Melissa, was in her mid forties she embarked on a second career teaching at a local university while working on a PhD. This was her lifelong dream. But after just a few years she noticed she was always tired and growing increasingly forgetful and disorganized. Her ability to teach began to suffer. Nothing seemed to help. Finally she was diagnosed with chronic Hepatitis C, which she had apparently been fighting for more than thirty years. Extreme fatigue and "brain fog" are among the most common side effects.

As with the cobbler's children who lack shoes, so too the pastor's spouse often goes without spiritual support. A sensitive pastor might have referred Melissa to these verses from the fourth "Servant Song" in the book of Isaiah, adopted by the early church to explain the mission of Jesus:

> Surely he has borne our infirmities
> and carried our diseases;
> yet we accounted him stricken,
> struck down by God, and afflicted.
> But he was wounded for our transgressions,
> crushed for our iniquities;
> upon him was the punishment that made us whole,
> and by his bruises we are healed.
> (Isa 53:4–6)

Melissa underwent forty-eight weeks of grueling treatment with Interferon and other medications. The virus rebounded a few months after treatment ended, and the resulting fatigue was worse than ever. So, at age fifty-seven, she had to leave her dream job and join the list of the disabled.

As she says now, "I'm lucky because I don't hurt. I just have to sleep and rest a lot, minimize stress and budget my energy very carefully. But it seems so cruel sometimes. I lost my abilities and I lost a huge part of my identity."

That same, more sensitive pastor, though acknowledging the depth of Melissa's loss, might have shared this sacred assurance from St. Paul:

> [Since] the Spirit of him who raised Jesus from the dead dwells in you, he who raised Christ from the dead will give life to your mortal bodies also through his Spirit that dwells in you.
> (Rom 8:11)

Disaster

As I write this, my home state of Alabama is reeling from a deadly outbreak of tornadoes. We are a tornado-prone region and are quite accustomed to the sound of the tornado sirens. When they sound the alarm, Psalm 57 gives us this prayer:

> Be merciful to me, O God, be merciful to me,
> for in you my soul takes refuge;
> in the shadow of your wings I will take refuge,
> until the destroying storms pass by.
> (Ps 57:1)

Some fifty tornadoes struck Alabama on April 27, 2011, killing more than 250 people, wiping out entire communities, disrupting thousands of lives, and causing billions of dollars in property damage. In the wake of any disaster, Psalm 46 provides assurance that divine help is on the way:

> God is our refuge and strength,
> a very present help in trouble.
> Therefore we will not fear, though the earth should change,
> though the mountains shake in the heart of the sea;
> though its waters roar and foam,
> though the mountains tremble with its tumult.
> There is a river whose streams make glad the city of God,
> the holy habitation of the Most High.
> God is in the midst of the city; it shall not be moved;
> God will help it when the morning dawns.
> (Ps 46:1–5)

When "morning dawned" in Alabama, the federal government and thousands of volunteers from around the nation began to descend upon Alabama. With this massive outpouring of aid our shattered state was assured that the words of Psalm 46 "are trustworthy and true" (Rev 21:5).

.

Divorce

MY FIRST marriage lasted twelve months to the day. Even though my sister says you don't have to count the short ones, I can tell you the pain was intense. I was embarrassed and ashamed of the failure, and my youthful fantasies of a political career seemed doomed.

The ancients didn't know about divorce American style," but they knew plenty about the pain of broken relationships. Consider these verses from Psalm 6:

> I am weary with my moaning;
> every night I flood my bed with tears;
> I drench my couch with my weeping.
> My eyes waste away because of grief.
> (Ps 6:6–7)

I had been unhappy as a single person, miserable as a married person, and bereft as "single again." Would that I had been able to summon this prayer from Psalm 69:

> I am lowly and in pain;
> let your salvation, O God, protect me.
> (Ps 69:29)

The sting of rejection is always painful, as it is often accompanied by resentment from real and/or imagined insult and injury. Where there is anger toward the other, Psalm 69 urges us to turn that hurt over to God and let God deal with it:

> Pour out your indignation upon them,
> and let your burning anger overtake them. . . .
> Add guilt to their guilt;
> may they have no acquittal from you.
> (Ps 69:24, 27)

Knowing God is on the case, we can then afford to be more civil to those whom we may feel have offended, betrayed, or rejected us.

Of course, the source of the problem may not be entirely with them. It may originate, in larger or in smaller degree, with us. Developing better self-awareness, we can move forward with this sacred assurance:

> Bless the LORD, O my soul,
> and do not forget all his benefits—
> who forgives all your iniquity,
> who heals all your diseases,
> who redeems your life from the Pit,
> who crowns you with steadfast love and mercy,
> who satisfies you with good as long as you live
> so that your youth is renewed like the eagle's.
> (Ps 103:2–5)

Note the promise of ultimate redemption: God "redeems your life from the Pit." You will get through this. Your hurt will be healed. Your emptiness will be filled.

> For [God's] anger is but for a moment;
> [God's] favor is for a lifetime.
> Weeping may linger for the night,
> but joy comes with the morning.
> (Ps 30:5)

Doubt

L IKE A bad cold, doubt is something that I suspect we've all had, and that many of us are destined to get again. Even Jesus, who cited Psalm 22 from the cross, had doubts:

> My God, my God, why have you forsaken me?
> Why are you so far from helping me, from the words of my groaning?
> O my God, I cry by day, but you do not answer;
> and by night, but find no rest.
> (Ps 22:1–2)

On Easter Sunday, encountering the risen Jesus on a mountaintop in Galilee, some of the disciples worshipped him, "but some doubted"(Matt 28:17). First Timothy concedes, "Without any doubt, the mystery of our religion is great" (1 Tim 3:16).

You could have fooled me! Why, I can remember the very first time I heard "God" and "mystery" in the same sentence. I was reared to think doubt was an unpardonable sin, for there was no mystery in matters of faith. From Genesis to Revelation, it was all fact. So, for many years I wondered what was wrong with me. Why could I not believe the claims of the Bible, the miracles, the supernatural wonders, the extraordinary accounts of divine rescue and redemption? Why could I not believe in God when belief seemed to come so easily to so many?

A chance encounter with a Dutch biblical scholar helped turn me around. I bought the book *Jesus*, by the late Edward Schillebeeckx, in paperback for $1.00 at a book sale. I bought it because in the dedication he quoted this verse from the Newer Testament: "that you may not grieve as others do who have no hope" (1 Thess 4:13).

Among the many things I learned from Schillebeeckx and other theologians is that in the biblical world the goal of faith is not belief, but hope: "Now faith is the assurance of things hoped for, the conviction of things not seen" (Heb 11:1).

For the poet of ancient Israel, faith hinges—not on believing the unbelievable—but on respect and hope:

> Truly the eye of the LORD is on those who [respect] him,
> on those who hope in [God's] steadfast love,
> to deliver their soul from death,
> and to keep them alive in famine.
> Our soul waits for the LORD;
> [God] is our help and shield.
> Our heart is glad in him,
> because we trust in [God's] holy name.
> Let your steadfast love, O LORD, be upon us,
> even as we hope in you.
> (Ps 33:18–22)

Family Discord

POPULAR MEDIA images notwithstanding, no family is exempt from the potential for discord: not the rich, not the poor, and certainly not those in the middle. Whenever domestic discord strikes, it can turn our world upside down. When that happens, Psalm 46 functions like a life raft on a stormy sea:

> God is our refuge and strength,
> a very present help in trouble.
> Therefore we will not fear, though the earth should change,
> though the mountains shake in the heart of the sea;
> though its waters roar and foam,
> though the mountains tremble with its tumult.
> (Ps 46:1–3)

Financial Woes

WHETHER THE national debt or the family finances, many of us worry incessantly over money. We do so despite the best advice of Jesus:

> Therefore I tell you, do not worry about your life,
> what you will eat,
> or about your body, what you will wear.
> For life is more than food,
> and the body more than clothing.
> (Luke 12:22–23)

Jesus goes on to urge,

> Consider the lilies, how they grow:
> they neither toil nor spin;
> yet I tell you, even Solomon in all his glory
> was not clothed like one of these.
> (Luke 12:27)

Well, you might say, those lovely lilies can look pretty because they don't have credit card debt, car notes, house notes, education debt, or medical bills. What about me? Jesus answers:

> And do not keep striving for what you are to eat
> and what you are to drink,
> and do not keep worrying.
> Instead, strive for [God's] kingdom,
> and these things will be given to you as well.
> (Luke 12:29, 31)

Grief

GRIEF AT the time of death is clearly acknowledged, even affirmed. But life is full of losses, as the ancients well knew. Loss of income, loss of meaningful work, loss of health, loss of companionship, even loss of a beloved pet— any one of these is a loss to be grieved:

> Be gracious to me, O LORD, for I am in distress;
> my eye wastes away from grief,
> my soul and body also.
> For my life is spent with sorrow,
> and my years with sighing;
> my strength fails because of my misery,
> and my bones waste away.
> (Ps 31:9–10)

The ancient poet of Israel is convinced that God takes note of our grief:

> Indeed you note trouble and grief,
> that you may take it into your hands.
> (Ps 10:14)

And St. Paul seeks to assure us that we do not grieve in vain:

> But we do not want you to be uninformed, brothers
> and sisters . . . so that you may not grieve as others do
> who have no hope.
> (1 Thess 4:13)

Heart Disease

BOTH MY father and my father-in-law suffered from heart disease, the leading cause of death in the United States. It is only natural to ask, What is God doing about this number-one killer? Psalm 10 answers for humble folks with weak hearts and other concerns:

> O LORD, you will hear the desire of the meek;
> you will strengthen their heart,
> you will incline your ear to do justice
> for the orphan and the oppressed,
> so that those from earth may strike terror no more.
> (Ps 10:17–18)

Congestive heart failure, the inability of the heart to pump enough blood to meet the body's needs, is a common, costly, disabling and potentially deadly condition said to strike up to ten percent of those over age sixty-five. Psalm 40 offers a prayer for those suffering with heart failure:

> My heart fails me.
> Be pleased, O LORD, to deliver me;
> O LORD, make haste to help me.
> (Ps 40:12c–13)

HEART SURGERY

In the tradition of Jesus, the Great Physician, surgeons in the United States perform thousands of heart operations every day. On the eve of surgery, it is only natural to have some anxiety, but the prophet Isaiah offers this assurance:

> Surely God is my salvation;
> I will trust, and will not be afraid,
> for the LORD GOD is my strength and my might;
> he has become my salvation.
> (Isa 12:2)

Every successful surgery is a modern miracle. Just imagine what a field day the ancient biblical writers would have reporting all of these miracles!

> Praise [God] for his mighty deeds;
> praise [God] according to his surpassing greatness!
> (Ps 150:2)

Illness in General

EVERYONE HAS something, some disease or disorder, some source of pain, weakness, anxiety, or limitation. We are mortal, not immortal beings. The Bible knows all too well that our bodies are susceptible to all manner of illness and injury. The prayer of good King Hezekiah is short and sweet: "Oh, restore me to health and make me live!" (Isa 38:16).

In the face of illness the ancient poet of Israel offers this sacred assurance:

> Bless the LORD, O my soul,
> and do not forget all his benefits—
> who forgives all your iniquity,
> who heals all your diseases,
> who redeems your life from the Pit,
> who crowns you with steadfast love and mercy,
> who satisfies you with good as long as you live
> so that your youth is renewed like the eagle's.
> (Ps 103:2–5)

Do you have questions? "Why me, Lord?" "Why is this happening to me?" You are not alone. God also has questions: "Is there no balm in Gilead? Is there no physician there?" (Jer 8:22a). What's more, God wants to know, "Why then has the health of my poor people not been restored?" (v. 22b). And Holy God makes extraordinary promises: "For I will restore health to you, and your wounds I will heal, says the Lord" (Jer 30:17).

Infertility

FOR A woman in the biblical world, infertility is as bad as it gets. It is a sign of disgrace. It is grounds for divorce. It pushes her to the outer margins of society, and even beyond. In three thousand years of biblical history, we know of only six previously barren women who experience the miraculous birth of a child. And yet, these six are enough to make the divine will known.

> [God] raises the poor from the dust,
> and lifts the needy from the ash heap. . . .
> [God] gives the barren woman a home,
> making her the joyous mother of children.
> (Ps 113:7, 9)

The women of antiquity would be absolutely astounded at the progress God is making on this front. According to the U.S. Centers for Disease Control, which collects the data, in 2009, there were more than 60,190 infants born through "assisted reproductive technology" (ART). So, why are some women who long for a child still left childless? I wish I could answer that question. All I can say is that we are mortal, not immortal beings. Our bodies are susceptible to a host of conditions and diseases.

> A voice says, "Cry out!"
> And I said, "What shall I cry?"

All people are grass,
their constancy is like the flower of the field.
The grass withers, the flower fades,
when the breath of the LORD blows upon it;
surely the people are grass.
The grass withers, the flower fades;
but the word of our God will stand forever.
(Isa 40:6–8)

And that word, God's last word, is always a word of hope: "faith is the assurance of things hoped for, the conviction of things not seen" (Heb 11:1).

Loneliness

EGOTISTICAL AS we humans are, we like to think that all of our problems are unique to our own time and place. Loneliness is one example. Surely, in the extended families, clans, villages, and tribes of antiquity, no one ever got lonely. Psalm 102 suggests we think again:

> I am like a lonely bird on the housetop.
> All day long my enemies taunt me;
> those who deride me use my name for a curse.
> For I eat ashes like bread,
> and mingle tears with my drink.
> (Ps 102:7–11)

"Enemies" may be personal or impersonal, illness or injury, the ravages of age or adverse circumstances, *but* . . . Remember, "but" is always the biggest word in faith:

> *But* you, O LORD, are enthroned forever;
> your name endures to all generations.
> (Ps 102:12)

Miscarriage and Death of a Child

WHILE A woman's greatest shame in the stories the Bible tells might have been the "failure" to bear a child, her deepest grief was surely the death of a child or children. We moderns have medical explanations for much of what the ancients attributed to fate or fault, but we can still find comfort in the ancient assurance that God knows the agony of parents who suffer the death of a child or children:

> Thus says the LORD:
> A voice is heard in Ramah,
> lamentation and bitter weeping.
> Rachel is weeping for her children;
> she refuses to be comforted for her children,
> because they are no more.
> (Jer 31:15, quoted in Matt 2:18)

Obesity and Battles with Weight

A STUNNING two-thirds of all Americans over the age of twenty are either overweight or obese, according to the National Institute of Health. And I am one of them! I exercise vigorously and eat mostly turkey sandwiches for lunch—only rarely 'burgers; never fries. And yet as the years go by my weight and my waist increase. Cookies and ice cream draw me like a fly to flypaper, and there I am stuck!

Thankfully, there are biblical resources for those of us battling the bulge, starting with the Twenty-third Psalm:

> The LORD is my shepherd, I shall not want.
> He makes me lie down in green pastures;
> he leads me beside still waters;
> he restores my soul.
> He leads me in right paths
> for his name's sake.
> Even though I walk through the darkest valley,
> I fear no evil;
> for you are with me;
> your rod and your staff—
> they comfort me.
> You prepare a table before me
> in the presence of my enemies;
> you anoint my head with oil;
> my cup overflows.

Surely goodness and mercy shall follow me
all the days of my life,
and I shall dwell in the house of the LORD
my whole life long.
(Ps 23)

Imagine being able to walk past the refrigerator reciting the opening line: "I shall not want" (v. 1). Imagine no more food cravings! Psalm 23 reminds us that God has set the table—a healthy table of fruits, vegetables, and grains: "He makes me lie down in green pastures; he leads me beside still waters" (v. 2). A healthy diet is the "right path" to which God leads us. Even though I walk through the "dark valleys" of temptation, "I fear no evil; for you are with me; your rod and your staff—they comfort me" (v. 4). "In the presence of my enemies"—fast food, sugary soft drinks, comfort foods, beer and wine—God "prepares a [healthy] table" of abundance: "my cup overflows" (v. 5).

Psalm 23 tells us that a huge reward awaits those who follow a health diet: "Surely goodness and mercy shall follow me all the days of my life, and I shall dwell in the house of the Lord my whole life long" (v. 6).

If only losing weight were as easy as quoting a beloved psalm. As it is, we're trapped in habits, lifestyles, and a culture that drives too many of us to eat too much and exercise too little. We need someone to go to mean old pharaoh and demand: "Let my people go" (Exod 5:1). When God first made that suggestion at the burning bush (Exod 3:1–9), Moses was in complete agreement. But when Moses learned God was tapping him for the job, Moses politely tried to decline (3:10–11). Not to worry, said God, "I will be with you" (v. 12). So it is that God taps each of us to get control of our own weight. No one else can do it for us. It is up to us, to be sure, but God promises divine help for this most difficult task:

> The LORD is my strength and my shield;
> in him my heart trusts;
> so I am helped, and my heart exults,
> and with my song I give thanks to [God].
> (Ps 28:7)

Parkinson's Disease

As a pastor, I failed a lonely woman named Margaret. I utterly and completely failed this victim of Parkinson's disease. Margaret was an aging, reclusive woman whom I had visited a few times in her small, ramshackle home. Relatives eventually placed her in a nursing home. That is where I saw her for the last time. She was lying on a bed in small room, her entire body racked with cruel convulsions. I whipped out my Bible and read,

> I consider that the sufferings of this present time are not worth comparing with the glory about to be revealed to us.
> (Rom 8:18)

Margaret responded in a voice stronger than any I had ever heard from her, saying, "I don't believe a word of it!" I was stunned, speechless. I can't remember how, or even if, I responded. Unfortunately for me, Margaret was dead before I could see her again. She would have been far better served by a pastor who could have assured her that God was aware of her suffering, having been alerted to this dread condition by the ancient poet of Israel:

> Be gracious to me, O Lord, for I am languishing;
> O Lord, heal me, for my bones are shaking with terror.
> My soul is struck with terror,
> while you, O Lord—how long?
> (Ps 6:2–3)

Margaret might have even found some consolation in knowing that one of the most famous characters in the Bible suffered similar tremors. Of course, for Daniel of lions' den fame the condition was brought on by entirely different circumstances. Even so, his testimony assures us that God knows the symptoms of Parkinson's disease.

> For I am shaking, no strength remains in me,
> and no breath is left in me.
> (Dan 10:17b)

Would that I could have assured Margaret of the same divine response Daniel receives:

> Again one in human form touched me
> and strengthened me.
> He said, "Do not fear, greatly beloved, you are safe.
> Be strong and courageous!"
> (Dan 10:18)

Physical Therapy

THE SURGEON says, "The procedure is routine; we do it every day. Expect a day or two in the hospital." He or she continues, "then we'll discharge you to physical therapy. It's a piece of cake." "Routine" and "a piece of cake" to the doctor, perhaps, but never to the patient.

Whether injury, surgery, stroke, or all of the above, the battle back is a hard-fought campaign for which the prophet Isaiah offers this encouragement:

> Those who wait for the LORD shall renew their strength,
> they shall mount up with wings like eagles,
> they shall run and not be weary,
> they shall walk and not faint.
> (Isa 40:31)

The poet of Israel seems to know physical therapy can be a long and arduous process. While one is limping around on crutches, using walker, or navigating in a wheelchair, scripture reminds us,

> [God's] delight is not in the strength of the horse,
> nor his pleasure in the speed of a runner;
> but the LORD takes pleasure in those who [respect] him,
> in those who hope in [God's] steadfast love.
> (Ps 147:10–11)

A daylong regimen of physical and/or occupational therapy can be exhausting, making these words of Jesus a welcomed assurance:

> Come to me, all you that are weary
> and are carrying heavy burdens,
> and I will give you rest.
> (Matt 11:28)

Sexual Abuse

THE NUMBERS are staggering. One out of every three girls, one of every eight boys will be sexually abused by the age of eighteen. Eighty to ninety percent of offenders are family members or someone close to the family. This is the case in the biblical story of King David's family. His daughter Tamar is raped by her brother Amnon, leaving her "a desolate woman" (2 Sam 13:20). When David refuses to punish Amnon for this despicable deed, another of his sons, Absalom, takes the law into his own hands and has Amnon killed (vv. 28–29). The first family of Israel comes apart at the seams, as is often the case when sexual abuse occurs.

What is God's word to the victims of abuse?

> [God] will wipe every tear from their eyes.
> Death will be no more;
> mourning and crying and pain will be no more,
> for the first things have passed away.
> (Rev 21:4)

And there is more from Jesus in the Sermon on the Mount:

> Blessed are the poor in spirit,
> for theirs is the kingdom of heaven.
> Blessed are those who mourn,
> for they will be comforted.
> Blessed are the meek, for they will inherit the earth.

Blessed are those who hunger and thirst
for righteousness, for they will be filled.
Blessed are the merciful, for they will receive mercy.
Blessed are the pure in heart, for they will see God.
Blessed are the peacemakers,
for they will be called children of God.
Blessed are those who are persecuted
for righteousness' sake,
for theirs is the kingdom of heaven.
(Matt 5:3–10)

By no means are "blessed are the meek" and "blessed are the peacemakers" to be taken as sacred signals for victims of abuse to keep quiet. Quite the contrary. When Jesus includes "hunger and thirst for righteousness" in his blessings, he is urging us to seek God's justice, which is key in halting the cycle of abuse that otherwise can spread from one generation to the next.

Stroke

WHEN JOANNE Fendley was felled by a stroke, she has just recently been named one of the "Unsung Servants" of the Presbyterian Church (U.S.A.). For more than fifteen years she had served her congregation as communion steward, preparing the elements of the Lord's Supper for worship each Lord's Day. In the blink of eye this humble officer of the church was blinking back tears of frustration over her inability to communicate her thoughts or to direct her limbs.

St. Paul confessed to similar frustrations. He called his condition a "thorn in the flesh." Having made three unsuccessful appeals for divine relief, the great apostle finally heard this response:

> My grace is sufficient for you,
> for power is made perfect in weakness.
> (2 Cor 12:9a)

With this assurance, St. Paul went on to set an example for all who suddenly find themselves dependent upon others:

> So, I will boast all the more gladly of my weaknesses, so
> that the power of Christ may dwell in me.
> Therefore I am content with weaknesses, insults, hardships,
> persecutions, and calamities for the sake of Christ;
> for whenever I am weak, then I am strong.
> (2 Cor 12:9b–10)

Working one's way back from the debilitating effects of a stroke can be a long and arduous process. With each agonizing step forward, stoke victims can take consolation in this sacred assurance:

> [God's] delight is not in the strength of the horse,
> nor his pleasure in the speed of a runner;
> but the LORD takes pleasure in those who [respect] him,
> in those who hope in [God's] steadfast love.
> (Ps 147:10–11)

Surgery

SURGERY IS serious. Certainly, any invasive surgery is fraught with danger. Scripture provides these words of encouragement for those about to "go under the knife":

> Be strong and courageous;
> do not be frightened or dismayed,
> for the LORD your God is with you wherever you go.
> (Josh 1:9)

When the report comes that the surgery was successful—"It was as big as a grapefruit, the size of an orange, but the doctor says they got it all!"—these verses help us celebrate:

> Bless the LORD, O my soul,
> and all that is within me,
> bless [God's] holy name.
> Bless the LORD, O my soul,
> and do not forget all his benefits—
> who forgives all your iniquity,
> who heals all your diseases, . . .
> who crowns you with steadfast love and mercy,
> who satisfies you with good as long as you live.
> (Ps 103:2–5)

When the results of surgery are not encouraging, the book of Psalms provides this prayer:

Be gracious to me, O LORD, for I am languishing;
O LORD, heal me, for my bones are shaking with terror.
My soul is struck with terror,
while you, O LORD—how long?
Turn, O LORD, save my life;
deliver me for the sake of your steadfast love.
(Ps 6:2–4)

Trouble

As I write this, early in the twenty-first century, the nation is in trouble: war on two fronts, rising budget deficits, stubborn recession, crime and overcrowded prisons. There is trouble at the statehouse: revenue is down, demand for services is up. There is trouble in the workplace: downsizing means layoffs for some, overwork for others. There is trouble at school: drugs, gangs, even guns. There is trouble at home: broken relationships, teenage pregnancy, and personal debt—plus, the car needs brakes and the dog has fleas!

The ancient poet of Israel is certainly no stranger to trouble. What is unique about the book of Psalms is how effectively the poet articulates those trials and tribulations directly to our Holy God. Here is an example:

> Though I walk in the midst of trouble,
> you preserve me against the wrath of my enemies;
> you stretch out your hand,
> and your right hand delivers me.
> The LORD will fulfill his purpose for me;
> your steadfast love, O LORD, endures forever.
> Do not forsake the work of your hands.
> (Ps 138:7–8)

Trouble comes as a shock to many, but to the ancient poet trouble is a given in the human experience: "Many are the afflictions of the righteous," concedes Psalm 34:19. But the same psalm offers this assurance, "The Lord is near to the brokenhearted, and saves the crushed in spirit" (v. 18).

"Take it to the Lord in prayer" is the advice of an old revival hymn. Psalm 13 gives us the words to do just that:

> How long, O LORD? Will you forget me forever?
> How long will you hide your face from me?
> How long must I bear pain in my soul,
> and have sorrow in my heart all day long?
> How long shall my enemy be exalted over me?
> Consider and answer me, O LORD my God!
> Give light to my eyes, or I will sleep the sleep of death,
> and my enemy will say, "I have prevailed";
> my foes will rejoice because I am shaken.
> (Ps 13:1–4)

Next comes, once again, that biggest word in faith: *but*. Having laid out the complaint to Holy God, having stated the case, the poet can now say,

> *But* I trusted in your steadfast love;
> my heart shall rejoice in your salvation.
> I will sing to the LORD,
> because he has dealt bountifully with me.
> (Ps 13:5–6)

Unemployment

"You're fired!" These are perhaps the harshest words ever spoken in the workplace. In our time, "the boss" has learned to soften the language—layoff, downsizing, and furlough—but not the blow. At such a time, Psalm 46 offers hope:

> God is our refuge and strength,
> a very present help in trouble.
> Therefore we will not fear,
> though the earth should change,
> though the mountains shake in the heart of the sea;
> though its waters roar and foam,
> though the mountains tremble with its tumult.
> (Ps 46:1–3)

Well-meaning people will tell you, "God has a plan," or, "This happened to fulfill a divine purpose." Maybe so, but God does not play human beings like puppets. The God of justice and mercy would never be the source of injustice or misery. However, Christians believe there is no situation out of which God cannot work good for God's people. Again, Psalm 46:

> There is a river whose streams make glad the city of God,
> the holy habitation of the Most High.
> God is in the midst of the city; it shall not be moved;
> God will help it when the morning dawns.
> The nations are in an uproar, the kingdoms totter;

[God] utters his voice, the earth melts.
The LORD of hosts is with us;
the God of Jacob [and Rachel and Leah] is our refuge.
(Ps 46:6–7)

Violence

GIVEN THE news in our time, one would think we moderns have cornered the market on violence: never-ending warfare, terrorism, drug cartels, street gangs, hardened criminals, sexual predators, and more. For the poet of Israel, however, this is nothing new:

> For I see violence and strife in the city.
> Day and night they go around it
> on its walls,
> and iniquity and trouble are within it;
> ruin is in its midst,
> oppression and fraud
> do not depart from its marketplace.
> (Ps 55:9b–11)

Yet Psalm 55 concludes with this expression of confidence in God's ultimate justice:

> But you, O God, will cast them down
> into the lowest pit;
> the bloodthirsty and treacherous
> shall not live out half their days.
> But I will trust in you.
> (Ps 55:23)

Where Do We Go from Here?

YOU HAVE made it through all of the above. Congra-
tulations! But where do we go from here? Permit me
to pass on this assurance:

> But I call upon God,
> and the LORD will save me.
> Evening and morning and at noon
> I utter my complaint and moan,
> and [God] will hear my voice.
> (Ps 55:16b–17)

In other words, keep on talking, keep on praying to
Holy God, remembering all the while that you are not alone:

> These things I remember,
> as I pour out my soul:
> how I went with the throng,
> and led them in procession to the house of God,
> with glad shouts and songs of thanksgiving,
> a multitude keeping festival.
> (Ps 42:4)

And this:

> I was glad when they said to me,
> "Let us go to the house of the LORD!"
> (Ps 122:1)

Popular culture idealizes the individual and individu-
ality. We seem never to outgrow the toddler's cry, "I can

76

do it myself!" We want to live on our own and to go when and where we choose. From 1776 to the present day, the American ideal is independence.

In great contrast, the biblical ideal is community: the twelve tribes and the twelve disciples, the ancient nation of Israel and the New Testament church. The Bible contends, "We're all in this together." And our ultimate hope, our redemption, will come to us as God creates, within the community of humankind, "a new heaven and a new earth":

> After this I looked, and there was a great multitude
> that no one could count, from every nation,
> from all tribes and peoples and languages,
> standing before the throne and before the Lamb,
> robed in white, with palm branches in their hands.
> They cried out in a loud voice, saying,
> "Salvation belongs to our God
> who is seated on the throne, and to the Lamb!"
> (Rev 7:9–10)

www.ingramcontent.com/pod-product-compliance
Lightning Source LLC
Chambersburg PA
CBHW071104090426
42737CB00013B/2475